2013   Jonina
Einars

RUNAWAY DREAMS

D0721507

Runaway Dreams

POEMS BY

Richard Wagamese

RONSDALE PRESS

RUNAWAY DREAMS
Copyright © 2011 Richard Wagamese

All rights reserved. No part of this publication may be reproduced, stored in a retrieval system, or transmitted, in any form or by any means, without prior written permission of the publisher, or, in Canada, in the case of photocopying or other reprographic copying, a licence from Access Copyright (Canadian Copyright Licensing Agency).

RONSDALE PRESS
3350 West 21st Avenue
Vancouver, B.C., Canada V6S 1G7
www.ronsdalepress.com

Typesetting: Julie Cochrane, in New Baskerville 11 pt on 13.5
Cover Design: Julie Cochrane
Paper: Ancient Forest Friendly Silva — FSC certified with 100% post-consumer waste, totally chlorine-free and acid-free

Ronsdale Press wishes to thank the following for their support of its publishing program: the Canada Council for the Arts, the Government of Canada through the Canada Book Fund, and the Province of British Columbia through the Book Publishing Tax Credit Program and the British Columbia Arts Council.

Library and Archives Canada Cataloguing in Publication

Wagamese, Richard
    Runaway dreams / Richard Wagamese.

Poems.
Issued also in electronic format.
ISBN 978-1-55380-129-0

    I. Title.

PS8595.A363R86 2011   C811'.54   C2011-903010-1

At Ronsdale Press we are committed to protecting the environment. To this end we are working with Canopy (formerly Markets Initiative) and printers to phase out our use of paper produced from ancient forests. This book is one step towards that goal.

Printed in Canada by Marquis Book Printing, Quebec, Canada

As always,
for Debra

ACKNOWLEDGEMENTS

—

One day in the early 1980s I showed some very bad poetry to the writer-in-residence at the Regina Public Library. I wasn't a poet. I just carried a lot of unhealed hurt and melancholy. But she helped me see where my writing could be stronger and in the end, wrote a blurb at the bottom of one of my hand-written pages, "Richard, you're going to do it!" So this first collection came about, almost thirty years later, because of Lorna Crozier, a great and wonderful poet. Thank you.

My wife Debra Powell makes everyday poetry. She offers me, every day, examples of a heart at work creating empowering and healing energy. I am always floored by that, rendered speechless, inarticulate and I can only stand in her light and be made more.

There are a host of friends to thank for making this possible: Pam and Bob Lee, Ron and Wanda Tronson, Ron and Jennifer Saint-Marie, Irene and Jon Buckle, Nancy and Peter Mutrie, Lee and June Emery, Tacey Ruffner, Kent Simmonds, Janet Whitehead, Cheryl Robertson, Dawne Taylor, Sarah and Byron Steele, Doug Perry, Tantoo Cardinal, Shelagh Rogers, Joseph Boyden, all the folks at Ronsdale, my agents John Pearce and Chris Casuccio.

Thanks also to my students in Writing 314 at the University of Victoria, and to Janet Marie (January) Rogers, who asked me one day if I had any poems — as it turns out I had a few of them.

"no one
not even the rain
has such small hands . . ."

— e.e. cummings
"Somewhere I Have Never Travelled"

CONTENTS

Poem

smoke tendrils roll upward
outward onward beyond
this abalone bowl bringing
the ancient ones
to stand at your shoulder
as the eagle feather fan
brushes smudge over the heart
and mind and spirit
making you a circle
containing everything
and nothing
at the same time

I can live like this
this being
blessed and blessing
in the same motion

the sacred medicines smoulder
drums
eagle cries
life
everything I hear

Paul Lake Evening

loon call wobbles over wind
eased through the gap between mountains
the lake set down aglitter
like a bowl of quartz winking
in the last frail light of sun
pushing colours around the sky

to sit here is to see this country
the way a blind man sees
the feeling of it all
pushed up hard against you
insistent as a child's hand
tugging at your sleeve

the Old Ones say
that everything is energy
and we're part of it
whether we know it or not

in the sky are pieces of me

we are the grass
alive with dancing
we are stone
vigilant and strong
we are birds
ancient with singing

the flesh of us
hand in hand, you and I
the whole wide world

He Dreams Himself

walking the line of the Winnipeg River
as it snakes northward out of the
rough and tangle of the Canadian Shield jutted
like a chin that holds Wabaseemoong
in its cleft and empties legends born
in its rapids and eddies of *Memegwaysiwuk*
the Water Fairies out of the belly
of Lake of the Woods

he dreams himself
talking to all the things he passes
singing their names sometimes
in the Old Talk
he won't awaken to understand

still, it's dream he walks through
and when he puts his hand upon
the pictographs set into stone
the iron oxide, bear grease
and pigment mixed to seal them
forever just above the waterline
on a cliff with no name
he feels the pulse of them on his palm
the sure, quick heartbeat of a thing
alive and captured squarely
in time, and wakes to find
his hand upon your hip bone
in the dim moonlight the stars
winking in a kind jest at the window

he dreams himself into being
as the Old Ones said
he would
in the teachings he holds as close
as you to the centre of himself

The Injun in this Poem

I

The Injun in this poem is planting flowers
kneeling like an acolyte at prayer
holding fragile life in his palms and wonders
looking up and around at this land
he's come to occupy at fifty-five how
he might have come to this shining
morning falling over half an acre
of mountainside with a digger in his hand
easing begonias and geraniums into earth
that dirts his fingers browner than they were
before he stepped outdoors into the flush
of light dappled by trees
containing birdsong and
wind song

the Injun in this poem holds the earth
up to his face and breathes the
musk and fungal fragrance that tells
stories of rock beings crumbled down to sand
and plant beings who surrendered themselves
in the Long Ago Time to become this rich
exhilaration of time and history cupped
neatly in his hand before easing it back down
using his fingers as a blade
to crater out a home for a new plant being
to become a hint of the chant that sings beneath
this eternal tale

the Injun in this poem is a hunter gatherer
hunkered down beside a ring of rock
that might have been a fire pit before
a Medicine Wheel or a ceremonial fire
where Grandfather stone
could scorch the ancient teachings
into his heart and mind and soul and take
him back into primordial time when this land
was still tribal land and the teachings sang
in everything and the idea of planting flowers
was unknown, considered nothing that
a native man would do, had no
need to do, when Creation
offered everything
but the Injun in this poem is planting flowers
happily, feeling much like a creator himself
in giving life a chance to express itself
this earth around his fingers becoming sacred
by virtue of his belief in it, his faith
that the teachings and the spirit
reside within it and that teachings come
over time to transcend even time itself
so that planting flowers becomes an Injun thing
by virtue of the Injun doing it
and believing it so

II

They say we cast our stories on the skin of birch trees once,
etching them there with the sharpened edge of a burnt stick
or pigments formed of earth and rock and plant material
that has never faded over time. I saw a birch bark scroll once.
The old man laid it out for me on a table top and traced a
line of history with one arthritic finger, telling it in the Old
Talk that I didn't understand. But I could translate his eyes.
In those ancient symbols was a world beyond worlds, of
legends alive, of a cosmology represented in the spirit of
everything, of teachings built of principles, built themselves of
rock and leaf and tree, bird and moose and sky, and Trickster
spirits nimble as dreams cajoling the Anishinabeg outward
onto the land toward themselves, toward him, toward me.
This is what I understood from the wet glimmer of his eyes.
This is what I carried away to here, to this page, stark in its
blankness, waiting like me to be imagined, to be filled.

III

The Injun in this poem stands washing dishes
looking out across a wide expanse of lake
and mountain while the sound of friends gathered
in the room beyond bubbles over jazz, Dvorak or the blues
and laughter like wavelets breaking over rocks
he wonders how this came to be
these nights when community happens of itself
and belonging is a buoyant bell clanging
in the harbour, the cove, the channel of his being

the way to here was never charted beyond
a vague idea of what might be possible if he were
blessed on one hand and lucky on the other
he did everything he could to break the charm
and he can laugh at that now, the folly of believing
in what he could convince himself as real
the task of being Injun not including

the spell of that charm, the lure of the desire he could never
state because he hadn't learned the language yet
and travelling incognito, silent as a thief
so that home was always the lighted path that led
off the sullen concrete of the streets and in the end
belonged to someone else, their lights
shining through the open windows where sounds
like those he hears behind him now came
to haunt him as he shuffled off into the night

the Injun in this poem nods to himself
wipes a bowl and sets it beside the other
dinner plates, the formal ones reserved for nights
like this that have no haunting overtones
"I'm from a nomadic culture after all," he says and laughs
hooks the towel on the rack and turns
into the current and joins the bubbling voices
in a room that belongs to him now

the nomad in his solitude
carried dreams of home

    IV

take
    this
        hand
            e x t e n d e d
curl its fingers in your palm
whisper to me now
tell me that night must pass

V

Medicine burns when touched by fire. The smoke and scent
of it climbing higher, curling into the corners of the room
where you sit watching it, following it with your eyes and a
feeling like desire at your belly and a cry ready at your throat.
There's a point where smoke will disappear and the elders
say this is where the Old Ones wait to hear you, your petitions
and your prayers, the Spirit World where all things return to
balance and time is reduced to dream. It vanishes. There's
a silence more profound than any words you've ever heard
or read and when you close your eyes you feel the weight of
ancient hands upon your shoulders and your brow and this
sacred smoke comes to inhabit you and in its burn and
smoulder, a returning to the energy you were born in —
and the room is filled with you.

VI

The Injun in this poem is talking
he's telling stories culled from a lifetime of travel
between worlds, between realities and ways of being
he's telling tales of desperate moons when his living
was like the harshest tribal winters with the howl
of the wind and the deepest freeze just beyond
the thin skin of a wigwam in the snow
he's spinning yarns of plenty when life provided life
and all he ever had to do was breathe as it was when
the Animal People came to offer up their flesh and teachings
so the Anishinabeg might survive and
travel forward to their destiny
he's telling spirit stories born of rock and water, air and sky
legends handed down from generations passed
and held in the hand like keepsakes
worn and rounded at the edges from use
he's offering anecdotes of everyone he's ever met
on the road of years that led him to this point in time:
Cree, Dene, Blackfoot, Metis, Ojib and Sioux

Hungarian, Finnish, Scot, Australian
Brit, Québécois and Swede
they all left him something to trundle down the road
and sort through later in private moments like luggage
he's recounting episodes of the serial drama
life became when choice was predicated on escape
harrowing nights of desperation drinking
and mornings blunt as dull axes
the hard clop of them against his chest
and then suddenly he's laughing like hell, knee-slapping crazy
telling everyone who'll hear it the folly
of it all and how in the end he discovered
that discovering himself meant everything he just said
so that now he's sombre, still as the pool of the sky
reflecting on the stories of a life told in hushed tones
around a fire with friends who see him as a shadow
and a light, become a Trickster too, somehow,
a teacher gambolling at the edges where the flames lick
darkness away and stories are born in the stark
cool caverns of the heart, stalactites mysterious everywhere
yes, the Injun in this poem is talking as he'll talk for years
story upon story creating landscapes out of living
like the Old Ones carving *dodems* out of wood
with something he's come to recognize as love

What Warriors Do

I never thought that I would see myself lugging armloads of wood through three feet of snow to pound my feet at the door of a cabin in the mountains to step into the warmth and crackle of a woodstove set in the corner of a living room with a window overlooking a lake where the gray of a February evening eases to a purple hung with stars. Never thought I'd see that. But then again I never thought I'd see myself banging nails and sawing wood, hanging pictures or planting flowers. I'm a warrior for God's sake. These hands are meant for fluting stone to points for arrows or for spears. For hauling gill nets out of water so cold the knuckles won't bend and for flaying back the skin of bear or moose or fighting back incursions, invasions, threats. That's what warriors do. Instead, I stand at the sink when dinner's done washing dishes, preparing the morning coffee, wiping counters and the table and making sure the dog gets fed. These rituals and small ceremonies I've come to. I never thought I'd come to see me looking at myself as something more than I have ever been or acknowledging that there is even more to the territory of my being than I have come to see so far. I'm older now and quiet feels better on the bones than noise and the only fight in me is the struggle to maintain it all, to keep it close to my chest, to give me another heart to beat against the cold. Never thought I'd see that. Never thought I'd welcome it. But these days the land beckons like highways used to and I've learned to step outside the door and be here, rooted to place, grounded, anchored by words like love and home that drop from my tongue like beads of light, shining, showing me the path to our door even through the darkest night where I've learned to listen to your breathing while you sleep. Touch you. Feel your skin against my palm and sing an honour song to the energy that wraps itself around us, surrounds us, protects us. I'd carry the world to you like those armloads of wood, one sure step at a time. That's what warriors do.

Ceremony

ceremony doesn't change you
the old woman said
you change you

ceremony
is just the trail
you learn to follow
until you reach the place
where that can happen

I became an Indian after that

Runaway Dreams

I ran away the first time when I was fourteen
sleeping in the cab of a rusted old Chev pickup
in an orchard outside of Beamsville
and waking to a morning purple as an old bruise
hungry, cold, lonely as a whipped pup
knowing I had to go back
but wishing strenuously
otherwise

I hit the road again at fifteen
and made it all the way to Miami Beach
the feel of the Greyhound wheels churning
through Pennsylvania like a hymn
and listening to an old black man in the Cincinnati station
sing me Bukka White songs with a tambourine
brought me more of the world in three verses
than I'd ever heard before

wandering Louisville
in the stark grey-green of morning
and realizing that Kentucky was more
than just the words of some old song
that it was people streaming to work
and the smell of fresh bread hanging in the air
somewhere like a tire on a rope
spinning and telling its stories to the breeze

then suddenly Knoxville
and the rippled blue promise of the Appalachians
while the guy beside me stank of old tobacco
and sipping Southern Comfort from a flask
talked of his home in the hills and how
Baltimore never really gave him a chance
to get his feet under him and make more
of things as he'd planned
for Ruth Ann and him
and the three kids
waiting

I kept repeating the name Chattanooga
to myself well into the red clay hills of Georgia
and there was something in the way Atlanta shone
with a hard resilient southern promise
that gave everything a sense of adventure
and hope so there was no room in my chest
for lonely or sorrow or melancholy or pain though
they were my constant partners then and I had
no wish for anything but the road
and the miles stacked up like a wall
between me and the bog of faces and smells
and recollections that had never once
meant anything like home was supposed to
in anything I'd read

from Lake City through Jacksonville
Daytona Beach and Fort Lauderdale
then swinging jauntily through Hialeah
into the shimmering pastel light of Miami
Florida was a dream unfolding like a map
I traced with a quivering finger against
the slick and polished windows
I splurged on sandals and a flowered shirt
and headed over the causeway to the beach
and stood gape-jawed and shaking at the glitter

of sand and surf and cocoa buttered bodies
and the push of cerulean blue
rinsing St. Catharines from my feet

I had paper route money
I'd taken from the bank
and it was enough to see me through a few days
and nights of sleeping on the beach near the breakwater
and the old hippies I met sharing wine and weed
singing Beatles songs, everyone caterwauling
the na-na-na Hey Jude part before downshifting
into "Let It Be," told me where there was a job
I could have if I could cook
up a good enough story and it turned out
I could and I spent a week and a half swamping
the floors of a cafeteria and bussing dishes until
I couldn't come up with a social security number
and they let me go with a handful of cash
and a sack of leftovers I carried to the beach
and joined in for a round of the goatskin
and a huff of the weed before seguing into
an emboldened version of "Me and Bobby Magee"

we stamped the streets of Miami Beach like rogues
swiping drinks from sidewalk tables careful
never to break a glass and laughing giddy
as only young fools can, never minding things
like hunger, rootlessness and a unique kind of lonely
that sets in on you when you see families together
ebullient in their joy of stepping forward into
the world joined by the hand and a look in the eye
that says "contentment" that jostles at your ribs

and one night talking
at the bus station counter with a motherly hooker
named Esperanza who fed me and made me
drink milk and eat an apple before turning me in
to the Border Patrol and telling me to go home
because I could die on those streets and kissing me
full on the lips the smell of her
all sweat and salt and jasmine
I carried north into the hard slant of winter wind
at the airport in Toronto
where it faded in the cut of eyes
waiting to get me home
and out of the public eye

there was no hope for me after that
the world had come up and flashed me
and shown me that there was more to it
than the brutal isolation of that house
and that magic existed in the open spaces
between buildings and people bent on
making something more out of something less
and all the runaway dreams —
they tried of course, to bend me to their rules
to discipline the Indian right out of me
and with every whack of the belt or hand
the bruises they made sure were
hidden well beneath my clothing
they'd look me sternly in the eye and say
"you'll never run away again" and I
would almost laugh out loud because
of course
I'd already left a thousand times
by then

Carnival Days — 1973

Riding the big rig out of South Cayuga
while headlights peel the skin off
Highway 3 leading you into Byng and Winger
then dipping south again into Wainfleet
with the smell of horses and cow dung
and fresh cut alfalfa. Timothy maybe, clover
and rain cutting north and west off Lake Erie

the sway of the fields so close
it felt like a sea
and the smell of grease and oil and rope
in the cab of the old Mack truck made you feel
like a mariner even though at seventeen
you'd only seen an ocean once
only ever felt adrift without a compass
or a pole star to lead you

so you pull into the town asleep
in the early morning wet
and stand shivering beside the rig
while other carnies drift across the lot
to stand beside the ride boss, smoking
smelling of last night's beer, cheap weed and two weeks
on the road without a bath and no one
says a thing, just stand there scratching
at their stubble or their ribs while the big man eyes the grounds
then grabs an arm of staves to mark the midway
marches it out in a matter of minutes and returns
to spit a stream of snuff at your shoes
and says "let's get 'er in the air"

you had no clue of what it meant to be Indian
then but it always struck you as a tribal sort of thing
that clanging, banging, sweating, cursing ceremony
of getting rides in the air
the lot of you bound by the carnie code
that says you work the show together
tossing wrenches, bolts and ball-peens between
the Tilt-a Whirl, the Octopus and Ferris Wheel
seeing whose crew could "get 'er done" first
then walking over to lend a hand elsewhere

so you heave and grunt in the hard sun
of another small town morning and try to ignore
the parade of hurly-burly village girls
trying to pretend they're not
the dip and swirl and thrust of young hips
eying the brown of you like a midway treat
edging closer and closer and asking questions like
"where ya from?" and "is that like, really heavy?"
and laughing, teasing, all rosy pink and clean
until you nod and smile and wipe the sweat and oil
from your face and start to promise rides
for free until someone's father grinds a smoke into the dirt
with the heel of a battered work boot and hollers "git"

you learned to live in a neon world back then
the flash and glitter of those lights all spin
and dance and synchronized and the wheel
turning slowly in the night above you
laughter falling like rain or confetti or the recollection
of dreams lying spent and sprawled, discarded
on the road somewhere behind you
people thanking you for transporting them back
to their own dreams of special girls, special boys
and long, wet first kisses while the wheel crested
throwing the whole midway into view
the light of it spectacular suddenly and them

giddy with the weightlessness of youth
the whole candy floss and candy apple world
rising like the ground to meet them

your world was roustabouts, semi-hacks and game-joint touts
and the smell of frying onions
from the grab joints down the way
and the creak and squeal of gears and turnbuckles
and cables taut in the wind that sent the dirt
in whirling dervishes to skittle across the apron
of the ride you swept clean fifty times a day
and the neigh of ponies in their harnesses
against the scream of someone's kid
frightened by the yawing mouth of a funhouse gargoyle
or a clown all brilliant and sad in the hard slash of sun
and the smell of sawdust in the rain
when the skies opened up and everyone came to huddle
under the awnings and smoke and cuss the luck
that sent the townies, the marks and the rubes packing
and the lingo of the lot was the argot of the road
where a town was a spot and a trip was a haul
and moolah was money except when you got specific
and what you really meant to say was
a fin, a sawbuck, a double or half a yard
the whole rambunctious, unpredictable
half-crazy, dizzily original
abstract landscape of it all set down hard against
sleepy, wink-eyed, dreamy small town Ontario
or Manitoba, Alberta or Quebec or wherever
that could come to feel like permanence almost
until the last ball or ring or dice was thrown
and the lot boss stood in the middle of it all
and yelled, "let's get this shit on the road!"

you'd tear it down just to build it again
a hundred miles down the road
and seventeen came to feel like a hundred sometimes
so that when you stood on the hub of the wheel
after bolting spokes and pulling cables snug
you felt the road and the miles and the wind
on your face and the feel of you
standing there suspended, thirty feet in the air
slowly growing older

Freddie Huculak

She's gone now the old Embassy Hotel. She used to sit on
the curve that dipped down into Port Dalhousie where we'd
go to sit and watch girls on the antique carousel and smoke
and drink and talk about cars and women and fights we'd
seen and he'd tell me about life on the boats and how the
St. Lawrence came to smell of everything that ever went to float
on her and how if you listened hard enough you could hear
those tales leaned over the rail in the fog come mornings
aiming for port. He told a good joke, too. He'd laugh like a
bastard and slap me on the back and pull me into it so that I
laughed too even though I didn't always understand what he
meant. I was just an under-aged kid slinging beer for seamen
for eighty bucks a week and living upstairs in a shitty room
beneath his, and hell, I needed heroes so bad back then that
a rough old tar was a blessing even if he was prone to two-
week speed benders and I had to talk him down sometimes
or get him out from under the bed when the paranoia drove
him into hiding and feed him soup and crackers and roll him
smokes and watch him while he shook when the turkey hit all
hard and fast. Still, he watched out for me. He'd bowleg into
the tavern, slap me on the back, and make a show for the big
boys that I knew somebody too tough to fuck with, then grab
a couple drafts and sit beside the shuffleboard to wait for a
game. He was a rough old bird. When I went to jail that first
time for fighting he said I only bought the time because I
won and if push came to shove in there to "eat mutton, say
nuttin'." He'd done a few stretches himself a few years back so
my twelve days were nothing but he was waiting when I came
back with a yellow ribbon wrapped around the doorknob to
my room and he laughed like hell when I saw it and then he
bought me a beer. "You're bigger than this," he said. "You got
more in you." I nodded even though I didn't understand what
he meant or saw in me and when I left there to chase summer

across Canada in a beat-up car I bought for a hundred bucks
he stood and watched and waved until I disappeared around
the curve. No one had ever waved goodbye before and I had
to hold tight to the wheel and set my chin to the country
and drive and drive and drive until the bruised feeling waned
into something grey and manageable. Almost forty years later
I think I understand. Bards sometimes sit in crummy rooms
scoffing a six pack and a hoagie, smoking roll-yer-owns and
waiting for the man to come with dreams in a baggie, betting
horses and drowning in old mariner tales. It's not all just
about glory and the shiny people who make it to the top.
What makes this country tick for kids like I was then are guys
like Huk, tough as hell and scrambling for a dollar, taking
love on the installment plan, givin' 'er the best they can and
letting young guys know they got better in them because
they learned somehow to see contrast through the gloom.
Well Huk, I got 'er now. Pass it on the best you can because
what you know is what you know, and you're a richer man
for seein' what you seen and a port in the fog is still a port.
If you're gone now and cold and reaching out for one last
beer, my guess is that you'll make it . . .

Tin Roof

I heard Fats Waller play one night
when the rain beat upon the slatted tin roof
of a cabin set against the rib of bush
somewhere beyond what I'd come to know as time

a wobbly candle flame
set the hornet's nest in the corner into motion
it danced in the magic of that night
that flame, that piano
and I fell in love with the 1920s
the simplicity of line and time and metre
and how it fit with rain
beating on a tin roof

a thousand tiny heartbeats like mine
surrendered to lonely

there are dreams that come to men as I was then
nomadic, transient, rootless, afraid perhaps
that time was like the road
always in front of you and never truly here
those dreams were visions and the quest of them
was what lifted a thumb to waggle and hook at cars
bearing hard for Winnipeg, Swift Current
then the foothills and the mountains tumbling down
to wide expanse of ocean
that was itself a dream dropped beyond the horizon
that itself was never really here

dreams of how the warmth of skin might feel
beneath a calloused palm
the cleft and cliff and scarp of bone
and hair and the smell of living
riding on each softly exhaled breath
in time suspended

and dreams of talk
the syllables of truth spilled off lips and tongue and teeth
to fill the air between us like clouds
roiling and turning and tumbling
with the energy of souls who have just discovered
that freedom rings best on turns of phrase that say
"I see you here" and "stay"

and dreams of lawns and things
the idle clutter that sits like islands in the stream of our living
redolent with history and song
like Waller's piano against the dark and the tattoo of rain
on that tin roof in the bush so far removed
from the light that breaks over things you've built
by hand
and heart
and hope

and dreams of time held in the hand
inspected with the gaping look of wonder
that you see on children's faces
when they become surprised by the ordinary

and dreams of sound and smell
the taste of things like the lilt of fresh baked bread
and the spot of skin just behind the ear
that holds within it the taste of many things
like faith and home and love
and the sound of spirits dancing in the ripple of curtains
in a window overlooking a yard
where flowers bloom in pots
where we dirtied our fingers and joined the earth to us again

I heard Fats Waller play as the rain pelted down
against an old tin roof and didn't know
that I dreamed of you

I can't hear that old piano now
without a sense of loss and celebration for this man
who found his way to you
down the road that led to the line in the sky
that led in course to the ocean
of our dreams come true
right here, right now, this room
where the feel of your skin against my palm
pulses like a simple line in a simple time and simple metre
like rain on the tin roof of my soul

Scars

The back of my head is pocked and marred
with scars I mostly don't remember getting
one time I fell in a drunken haze
against rocks along the Bow River
and opened myself severely
no stitches though, that would have been weak
and two-fisted gulpers as I was then
had no time for namby-pamby baby things
like doctors, anesthetic or thread pulled taut
in a seam to stem the flow of blood
I wear my hair short these days
and new barbers comment on the bare field
of it beneath the hair like a landing strip for pain
"musta been a whack" they say
and me in not so subtle denial have been
known to say "yeah, but chicks dig it"

the truth is
that I don't know that they do
bad boys create their own mythologies
in order to cope with frailty and failings
as though faulty legends and tall tales could replace
the truth of things in matters of the heart
Paul Bunyan outranks Tiny Tim
in our minds only and women get that
and it's the measure of our lack
that buffoons as I was didn't

I do now
but of course, I'm far more sensitive at fifty-five
than I was at twenty-three and time has a way
of bringing you to your knees
at the shrine of your own undoing

hell, even outlaws learn to cry if they listen
to themselves long enough
and there are a lot of cellblocks with tear stained pillows
clenched in tattooed fists

anyone or anything I ever fought
was only me in disguise
I get that now just as I've learned
that reaching out takes a lot more guts
than pushing away
and tall tales are better saved for firesides
when hurt's involved

there are scars from knives and bats and fists
that create a map of everywhere I fell
without knowing that I did
and there are scars from falling on broken bottles
careless work with tools and simple
drunken buffoonery that I eased with lies
because the truth was so embarrassing

my skin is broken territory
and my heart went along for the ride

but I've learned to see my scars as something
far more telling than the fables and tall tales
I created just to manage having been an idiot
more than a handful of times over time
because stitches and the billboards of bare spots
only mark the places I deserted myself
in my search for rest

outlaws in their hideouts dream
of a gentle touch and curtains
far more often
than they give away

Grammar Lesson

There's a silence words
leave in their wake
once they're spoken
that's the true punctuation
of our lives

like
when I said "I love you"
the full colon stop
made my heart ache
until you continued
the phrase and said
        dash
"I love you too"

period

Voyageurs

for Anne Doucette and Michael Findlay

Dvorak wrote the "Serenade for Strings"
in just twelve days and trudging through
the snow drifts along the bluffs above
the North Saskatchewan River with Saskatoon
huffing its breath across the frozen fling
of it in the valley, the violas sashay
in waltz time through the headphones
and I tuck my chin closer to my chest
and walk in counterpoint to the edge
and gaze in rapt wonder at the skill of
this Czech composer and the hand of Creator
at work together in the same morning
twinkling with frost

the river current buckled ice and sent
shards of it upward hard into a January
sky pale blue as a sled dog's eye
and the ice crystals in the air wink
in the sun like spirits dancing
so that Dvorak's masterpiece becomes
a divertimento to the history that clings
to the banks of this river and there's
something in the caesura that harkens
to a voyageur's song perhaps when
this river bore stout-hearted strangers
into places where only the Cree
and the buffalo could last the bitter
snap of the Long Snow Moons
and starvation was the only verb
in a language built on nouns

crows hop across the drifts
like eighth notes and the larghetto
when it eases in as wistful as a
prayer for home becomes the idea
that we're all voyageurs really
paddling relentlessly for points beyond
what we've come to know of ourselves
and time and the places we occupy
so that history whether it comes
in a serenade, a fugue, a chanson
or a chant sung with drums
made of deer hide becomes
the same song eventually and rivers
like this contain it
hold it, shape it to us
so it rides loose and easy
on our shoulders

Dvorak wrote the "Serenade" in 1875
and turning to the city now
marching to the beat of the teeth
of the wind that churns upward
suddenly out of the valley
Saskatoon becomes the everywhere
of my experience and I ride the current of it
to the resolution of the theme

Paul Lake Morning

from the deck you watch over coffee as everywhere
shadow surrenders to light
there's a motion to it, a falling back
as though the world were being pushed
into daylight shapes again
the boundaries of things assuming
their more familiar proportions
so that from here you get the sense of the universe
shrugging its shoulders into wakefulness
all things together

you come here to be part of it
this ceremony of morning, this first light
they call *Beedahbun* in the Old Talk
you can feel it enter you
the light pouring into the cracks
and crevices of your being
even with your eyes closed the wash
of it like surf against your ribs and the air
crisp as icicles on your tongue

there's gentleness in this slow sure creep into being
and something in you reacts to that
needs it, wants it, dreamt it sometime
so that the sun's ebullient cascade
down the pine-pocked flank of mountain
becomes the first squawk and natter of ravens
in the high branches of fir where the wind
soughs like the exhalation of a great bear
raising her snout in salute and celebration
to this Great Mystery presenting itself again

Nindinaway-majahnee-dog is what the Anishinabeg say
and when that language was reborn in you
that phrase more than anything adhered to your insides
all my relations
this is what you see from here
this connectedness to things, this critical joining that becomes
a revelation, a prayer and an honour song all at the same time
a blessing, really, that someone cared enough
to come and find you in your wandering
and bring you home to it, to ritual, to history
to language and the teachings you've learned to see
and hear and taste and feel and intuit in everything
this ceremony of becoming
that morning brings you to again

you become Ojibway
like the way you become a Human Being
measure by measure, step by step
on a trail blazed by the hand of grace
every awakening a reclaiming of the light
you were born to

The Canada Poem

I

Listen. Can you not hear the voices of the Old Ones talking,
speaking to you in the language you've forgotten? In your
quietest moments can you not feel the weight of an old and
wrinkled hand upon your shoulder or your brow? Listen.
Close your eyes and listen and tell me if you cannot hear the
exhalation of a collected breath from your ancestors in the
spirit world standing here beside you even now. Listen.
They are talking. They speak to you in Dene, Cree, Micmac,
Blackfoot, Ojibway and Inuktitut but they also speak
Hungarian, German, Gaelic, Portuguese, French, Mandarin
and English. The voices of the Old Ones. The ones who
made this country speak to us now because there is no colour
in the spirit world, no skin. Just as there is no time, there is
no history. There's only spirit, only energy flowing outward,
onward in a great eternal circle that includes every soul that's
ever stood upon this land, embraced this Earth, been borne
forward on this Creation and then fallen head over heels in
love with the spell of this country. Listen. They are speaking
to all of us now, telling us that we're all in this together — and
we always were. Listen. Only listen and you will hear them.
They speak in the hard bite of an Atlantic wind across Belle
Isle, in the rush of Nahanni waters, in the pastoral quiet over
Wynyard, in the waft of thermals climbing over Revelstoke
and Field to coast down and settle over Okotoks, then again
in the salt spray of Haida Gwaii, the screech of an eagle over
the wide blue eye of the lake called Great Bear and in the
crackle, swish and snap of Northern Lights you can hear in
the frigid air above Pangnirtung. They speak to us there.
Listen. Listen. There are spirit voices talking, weaving threads
of disparate stories into one great aural tapestry of talk that
will outlast us all — the story of a place called Kanata that has
come to mean "our home."

II

sitting with Earl in the cab of his truck
the '65 Mercury all banged to hell
from running woodlot roads and hauling
boats and motors through bogs and swamps
to landings the Ojibway said were there
and where the jack and pickerel lurked
in the depths beyond the bass at the reeds
"more'n yuh could shake a stick at," he said
and laughed and rubbed a calloused palm
along the windshield and talked about how
"this old girl, she done seen her day but she
still got go in her by god" and laughs again
and talks about his wife and him
coming here in the late summer of 1949
fresh off failed farmland outside of Milton
and determined to find waters like those
he fished as a boy in Finland and laughs
and tells me about pike longer than his arm
pulled out of the Ruunaa Rapids
and how this country here takes him back
even the smell of it he says and that's why
they come to build a fishing lodge here
because the Nipigon River runs like the
River Lieksanjoki of his youth and "by god
we got brook trout break da goddam arm sometimes"

he tells of building the lodge on the rocks
above a wide bend in the river
and how his wife came to love the feel
of the wind on her face those nights
when the work was done and she'd sit
in the willow rocker he built her
set under the eaves on the rough-hewn deck
and sing him Finnish folk songs
while he sat drinking tea and staring
out across the sweep of land

that reminded him so much of home
until one by one the stars winked
into view and they would move into the house
to lie awake to watch the moon shadow
creep across the log walls until sleep came and swept
them both away to Kuopio and the waters
they still loved as much as these

Anna-Liisa he says quietly and rubs
at the corner of an eye before he speaks again
she passed away three years before I met him
and he talks of laying her to rest
beneath the towering pines that hung
above the cleft of pink granite where
she planted wildflowers in the cracks and crevices
and he set that old willow rocker on those rocks
so he could go out of an evening and sit
and talk to her and sing old Finnish folk songs
while he watched the sun go down
"it's her land now by god" he says
"and my land too because of where she sleeps"
and there's nothing I can say but nod and smoke
and stare at the Nipigon River rushing south
beyond the peninsula and out into
the broad purple dream of Lake Superior
we ate sardines and crackers and drank warm ale
in the cab of that beat-up truck
and he asked me questions about myself
that I didn't hold the answers to and he
would nod his head and rub the dashboard
in small gentle circles with the pad
of one finger and smile sadly
"I come here to find myself" he said
"and it was not even yet my home
and here it's been yours all along
and still we make the same journey"

he dropped me off outside of Thunder Bay
in the chill and wet of morning
handed me thirty crumpled dollars
and said "come back and work by god"
and waved and drove away for food
supplies and a host of Finnish friends
and I stood alone
on the shoulder of another deserted highway
waiting, that summer of '74, and wishing
that I might make it back someday but
both of us knowing
that I never would

III

in Shebandowan the miners drive
their Cats into town to drink
with Ojibway kids
on the run from Kaministiquia
or Shabaqua or Atitkokan
roll them cigarettes one-handed
tell them horror stories of the mines
then let them win at pool
so they can get them drunk and laugh

there's something about a D8 Cat
that gives a man a sense of power
and maybe that's what they chase
so they don't have to think
of home and women and kids
or ordinary shit like that
they drink as they live
hard and fast, two-fisted
as if they could blow the foamy head
from all the tomorrows
and never heed the darkness
that walks with them
in the depths

instead they sit and drink and cuss
arm wrestle and brag
and leer at the Indian girls
until someone hollers "squaw"
and the fight breaks out

well, I heard all their stories
then I drank their beer for nothing
before kicking ass at pool
and thumbing out of town
with a pocketful of their money

IV

Riding out of Elkhorn with a gang of transients in the back of
a stake truck after stooking wheat for ten days in the Manitoba
heat. There's easier ways to make a buck but you take what
you can get when the Rambler Typhoon breaks down in the
middle of nowhere and the Mounties shake you awake by the
foot sleeping behind the Esso and give you the choice of "jail
or job." Still, the food was good and when the guy beside you
asks you for a smoke you give him one because he told a real
good one about Cape Breton one night around the fire that
made you laugh like hell. The gang of you headed west.
Their names are gone but you recall the places: Come By
Chance, Sissiboo Falls, Moosehorn, Snag and Wandering
River. They were Russian, French, German, English, Inuit,
Swede and Blackfoot and everyone came with stories that
crackled with the light of the fire outside the bunk house
and there were songs sung all guttural and low while goatskins
got passed along with the last of someone's hash and you
could look up and see the moon hung like a blind man's eye
throwing everything in that prairie night into a mazy, snowy
blue that made each of those tales a portal you stepped
through as easily as breathing until the voices stilled and
the fire died and the lot of you stumbled to your bunks to
dream of better days somewhere beyond the dry rasp of wheat

and the press of heat like an iron to your back and clouds of
chaff in your nose. You smoke and watch the land sail by and
wonder where you'll land next and someone bumps your foot
with the toe of a broken shoe and grins and you hand off the
butt and watch him lean his head back against the wooden
slat and exhale long and slow, the cloud of it vanishing back
behind the truck like dreams born somewhere you never
heard of before.

V

She kept an old and battered Bible
on the table made of packing crates
and drank Indian tea from metal cups
poured from a pot dangled
over a birch log fire
in the stone hearth that held
black and white photos of her children
and her husband all long gone
the edges scalloped, curled and yellowed
and medals from the Indian school
for penmanship and spelling

she lived in Eden Valley
in the shadows of the foothills for so long
she said, the hills became her bones
and she watched the reservation change
as the Old Ones like her died away
and the young ones drifted off
chasing city dreams and left their talk behind

but she taught me how to build a sweat
and sing an honour song to the breaking
day and to lay tobacco down when
we walked across the land to gather
the sweet grass and the sage
she taught me how to pray with

"always ask for nothing" she told me
"just give thanks for what's already here,
that's how an Indyun prays"

she told me stories
legends and amazing tales
of creatures and spirits and times before
things changed forever for the Stoney
and how the nuns at the residential schools
taught them how to scour everything
even the Indian off themselves
"then why the Bible?" I asked
and she smiled and took my hand
in both of hers like elders do
"because Jesus wept" she said

it took me years to finally get it
and when I did I looked up to the sky
and said thanks for everything that was
and is and ever would be
because Jesus wept
in gratitude for pain
and the salvation that comes
with the acceptance of it

when you learn to hold it
you can learn to let it go
it's how an Indian prays

VI

Looking out across the lake and seeing
how the mist seems to hold it all together
so that even the loon calls seem connected
to the side of the mountain standing
tall and proud as a chief
or a medicine woman
the forest dropping to the shore
like the fringes of buckskin the stone
of the cliff at the turn of the lake
a shining bead in the flare of the rising sun

it all comes together of its own accord
and all you can do is stand here
and take it in and hold it like a breath
you never want to exhale
these radiant shining moments
that have come to be the foundation
of your time here

when you think of this country now
it becomes as perfect as this vista
this lake and these mountains stunning
in the magnitude of the force of them
resting together on the power of detail

like when you watch your wife cutting
glass for the art she forms with a kiln
seeing how the minute bits of silica
fused together become something more
by virtue of the vision she has
of their wholeness

her story began on a convict ship bound
for the shores of Western Australia
and continued in the buying and the selling
of her great-grandmother on a Fremantle dock

a West Indian black whose face you see
in the line of her face when the light
catches it just so or the direct way
she has of looking at you telling you
with the strength of that level gaze
that the chains that bind her to the past
are forged from love and the knowledge
that her story, her life, is not just what
you see but the sum of its parts
like a lake shining at the foot of a mountain

your story began in a residential school
in northwestern Ontario where your family
was hung upon a cross of doctrine
that said to save the child they must
kill the Indian first — and did almost
except that you were born
in a canvas army tent in a trap-line camp
set beside the crooked water of the Winnipeg River
tucked in a cradleboard on a bed of spruce and cedar
hearing the Old Talk cooed and whispered
by the grandmother who could not save
you in the end from being
scooped away and taken to a white world
where the Indian was scraped away
and the rawness and the woundings
at your belly seeped and bled
their poisons into you for years

both of you adopted
removed
from the shelter of arms
that held you first
the story of you edited
by crude punctuation

and the journeys that you took from there
led you to extraordinary places of dark
and light and all shades in between
the acts of discovery and reclamation
adding to the image you hold now
both of you willing to tell it to each other
so that you know that what makes you stronger
is the coming together of those stories
the union of your lives the harmony that happens
when the weave of things is allowed to blend
all on its own accord
a confluence of energy and spirit
that the Old Ones say occurs without any help from us
the detail of things defined by Creator's purpose
and fused together into wholeness
like a lake shining at the foot of a mountain

so you look across this stretch of Canada
and it's as if you can feel the whole of it
shimmer beneath your feet like the locomotive
thunder of a hundred thousand hooves of buffalo
charging into history
or the skin of a great drum beating
carried in the feet of young men dancing
grasses flat for the gathering of people
come to celebrate the sun
and the wind that blows across the water
becomes the same wind that blew across
the gritty, dusty faces of settler folk freed
from the yoke of Europe the tribe of them
following the creak of wagon wheels
forward into a history shared
by diverse peoples with wondrous stories
told around fires
that kept them sheltered from the night

so maybe this is what it comes to mean
this word, this name, this Kanata
the Huron word for village that has
come to mean "our home"
maybe in the end it's a word for one fire
burning where a circle of people gathers
to hear the stories that define them

VII

Listen. They are with us. They are standing with us even now,
at your shoulder while you gather nets, forge steel, harvest
crops, lay roads, build houses, tend homes, raise children
or stalk moose through a muskeg bog. Can you not feel the
comforting presence of them watching over you? Can you
not feel the weight of an old and wrinkled hand upon your
shoulder or your brow? They are with us whether you believe
in them or not. The Old Ones. The ancestors. Spirit Beings
who have travelled onward, outward into the Spirit World
bearing with them the memories, the recollections and the
love they found here in this world, on this land, hovered over
you, telling you by the gift of intuition that they are here and
always will be. Can you not feel the truth of that? We are the
story of our time here they have come to say, and in the end
it is all we carry forward and all we leave behind. Our story.
Everything we own. Spin a grand tale then. Separately but
together leave the greatest story that you can for those who
come behind you. This is what they say and this is what they
wish. Nothing is truly separate. Every one and every thing
carries within it the spark of Creation and exists on the sacred
breath of that Creation. So that we are all related, we are
family, we are kin. Every story carries within it the seed of a
thousand others and it is only in the coming together that
we discover the truth of that and know that we are home.

Elder 1

At night he'd sit and smoke an old cob pipe
the glow of it in the dark throwing
his face into orange cliffs and dark canyons
of knowing with each drawn breath
like how a September wind can
freeze a man's face in the channel
between Minaki and Gun Lake or how
a cattail root can keep a man alive
when there's nothing else
or how to boil a cedar root
to fashion rope and waterproof the seams
of a tent or a canoe with the residue

sometimes he just talked
and the roll of it would carry me
beyond this world into the places
where stories are born
and a culture sprang from what
a storyteller saw in the shape and form
of a rock, say, or the shadow thrown
by the lean of a tree

it wasn't teaching
not in the strictest sense

he offered his experience
a canvas tent set among the trees
overlooking a cove at One Man Lake
where a fire burned in a pot-bellied stove
and the smell of cedar boughs and spruce
wafted through the aroma
of hard black tea and sweet grass
and the aged ones sat on stump chairs
grinning at you all awkward in the doorway
saying "*peendigaen, peendigaen*"
come in, come in

he'd talk for hours sometimes
and when he was finished
he'd take one last draw on the old cob pipe
and the light would flare like a tribal fire on a distant hill
then I'd hear him thunk it on a log and rise
to shuffle off to his tent
and allow the night to fall

Grandfather Talking — Whitedog Dam

them they didn't know
how much they come to hurt us with that dam
never seen how it could be

they just come and built their concrete wall
and stopped that water, pushed it back into a lake
where Creator never intended no lake to be
and them they never knew it was our blood, our life
was just a river to them, just a thing they could use
and they watched as the land got swallowed up by it
all the trees, all the rocks that marked
the end of one family's trapline from another
and the teachin' stones where our grandfathers painted
visions and prayer songs there
all drowned and covered up from our view
so that a part of us was drowned forever too

but them they never seen that

all them sacred places got washed away
not the big ceremonial places I mean
I mean them places where the hearts of our people
come to live forever
the bend above the rapids where I stretched my nets
when I was young and where I kissed your Gokum
that first time, oh that was a good one that one
so good, my boy, I felt that river inside me then
deep an' cool it was and me I felt like

I was never gonna be thirsty no more on accounta that kiss
and that bend in the river there
that's the kind of places they let sink away
spirit places I mean to say
where our spirits come alive, each of us, all of us
where we learned to live

them they never seen that

all they seen was that dam them
the push of the river against them big wheels inside
bringin' out what they call the hydro
but the word they use for it is power
and them they couldn't see that
that was what they drowned

Fresh Horses

Out of the alleys rumpled kings emerge
rolling cigarettes cadged from butts one-handed
and hitching up their pants with the other
wheezing, gasping, coughing
spilling onto the street on a morning
grey as campfire smoke — the remnants
of last night or yesterday slung on their lips
in drool or a snarl, shaking like a dog shitting razor blades
for another hit, another fix, a drink, an eye-opener
is how they call it

one by one the assemblage of pain
emerges from the holes and shadows
where they've hunkered in or hunkered down
and the street becomes a loose parade
marching back and forth between
a smoke and the feral early-morning dealers
slinging someone else's product for enough to start the trip
    themselves

wheelmen push their carts along behind
the dumpster divers scratching for scraps

you'll eat anything when you're starved enough
you can even nudge the rats aside
if there's enough for both of you

broken women with wild eyes
and skimpy dresses swiped off Army & Navy racks
slink in and ply what remains of their charm and wiles
for a taste, a hit, a drag, a smile even
if it might mean twenty dollars later
when everyone's looped and stranger things

have happened than a furious hump in the alley
between friends and a good ten rock

passersby have learned to walk the line
that exists two feet away from the edge of curb
where you can't be grabbed or sprung upon
or where it takes a good determined lurch to reach you
so that there's an open lane of concrete
between worlds like a land claim where
they've learned to stick to their side of the deal

there's cowboys and Indians, space cadets and hippies
sidewalk commandos and bikers without bikes
and someone's college sweetheart holding hands
with a rancher's son who dreams of horses
out beyond the derricks of Alberta grazing
with only the wind for company and the sun
shone down upon it all resplendent
as memories when they vanish in the wash
of this life, the tide of it beyond
all knowing

he dreams of horses
the roll of them beneath his butt and thighs
and the land swept by in the push and punch
of hooves and snorted breath across
the hard pan prairie and how it feels sometimes
to run them hard as far as they can go
before climbing on a fresh one
and kicking it to a gallop that pulls the foothills
closer

"We need fresh horses," he mumbles to her
but she can only squeeze his hand and squint
into the near distance
on a morning hard as stone

Urban Indian: Portrait 1

he stands at the corner
looking through the tangle
of one braid undone
the nest of it falling
against his cheek
while he toes
the butts at his feet
shrugs and stoops and fingers
one to his lips
like a desultory kiss
then flares the match
and sighs
the day into being

Urban Indian: Portrait 2

she sits in the window
overlooking Pigeon Park
and eases silken fringes
between arthritic fingers
the shawl her grandmother
gave her at the Standing Buffalo powwow
the year before she died

fancy dancing spinning
kicking pretending
the drum could push her
floating across the air
she touched down here
many moons ago
the faded outline
of the Saskatchewan hills
sketched in the wrinkles of her brow

she doesn't dance now
can barely walk
but staring down at derelicts
hookers, junkies, drunks
and other pavement gypsies
she sings an honour song
so that their ancestors might
watch over and protect them

the same song
her grandmother taught her
to sing in the shawl
snug about her shoulders

Urban Indian: Portrait 3

he stares across a vacant sea
of asphalt and pulls both hands
across his belly slanted
to his hip
and recalls the great canoe

they paddled out of Kitimat
then down Hecate Strait
and into Queen Charlotte Sound
the summer he was twelve
and he can still feel the muscle
of the channel on his arm
the smell of it
potent, rich, eternal
the smell of dreams and visions
thunderbirds dancing
orca chasing raven
across the slick surface
of the sea

he crosses to his closet
and retrieves the tools and wood
and paints he stores there
bundles it in the button blanket
he danced in once
and heads down the stairs
out into the street
to find the kids
he teaches to carve paddles now

the ocean
phosphorescent
in the moonlight
what he brings to them

Grandfather Talking 2 — Teachings

me I never thought that bein' Injun
was any diff'rent than someone else
we see the same sky, breathe
the same air, feel the same
earth under our feet
and everyone smiles with the sun on their back
an' the cool wind on their face

us we never knew no better
than what our teachin's told us
and what they say is that us people
swim out into the world the same
born innocent us, all of us
needin' help and shelter and warm
skin against our own to tell us
that this world outside our mother's belly
beats with one heartbeat
like the drum of her heart
we heard in darkness

that's what teachin's are meant to do, my boy
lead us back to that one heartbeat

me I remember once long time ago
when I was small maybe nine, maybe ten
when we still lived the trap line life
thirty miles out near One Man Lake
where the *manomin* grew thick as the bush
in the coves an' bays near our tents
and I could hear it rustle in the wind at night
in my blankets on a bed of cedar boughs
me I went to sleep all summer hearin' that voice
like a whisper in my ear all night long
the promise of the rice
filling up my dreams

anyhow my grandmother says to me one day
it's time for me to be a man an' me
I thought I was gonna get to hunt
get my first bear, first moose, first deer
but she took me walkin' through the bush
an' made me gather sticks and dry wood
to carry back to camp
an' said that I was gonna be the fire-keeper now
oh, me, my boy, I wanted to hunt so bad
and makin' fire didn't seem no warrior kind of thing
to me an' I made a big sad face at her

well her she sat me down beside her
and never said nothing for the longest time
until she raised a hand and pointed around our camp
"see the Old Ones," she said to me
"see how they sit close to that fire to warm their bones?
see how they like that lots?"
me I seen that and it made me smile

"see them young ones," she said
"see how they run to that fire for their soup
see how happy in the belly they are?"
I seen that too me

"tonight," the old lady said
"the storyteller will sit at that fire and us
we'll sit there too and hear the voice of magic in the night,
that fire throwin' sparks like spirits
flyin' in the air all around us all
and us we'll feel happy in that togetherness
like we done for generations now here
on the shore of this lake with the sound
of the wind in the trees like the sound
of the Old Ones whisperin' our names."

me I seen that too an' I looked at her
and my face wasn't so big and sad no more

"you bring the fire here," she said
"you light the flame where we gather
an' you cause all that to be, my boy
you take care of us that way
keep us warm, keep us fed, keep us happy
every stick you gather is a part of that
a part of learnin' how to care for us
and when you learn how to do that good
your grandfather will come
and show you how to hunt."

me I never forgot that
and I learned to be a fire-keeper
before I learned to hunt and trap and net
that's how the teachin's work, my boy
learn them slow and they become you
and you in turn become them too
more Anishinabeg, more Injun, more human being
and by the time you turn around on that path
to look back on where you come that's when you get to see
that you learned the biggest thing first
to care for people
to light a fire in the night
for them to follow home

and us we're all the same us people
guess we're all Injun that way us humans
we tend to that one heartbeat that joins us up
like we tend a fire to keep our people warm
and fed and happy

the teachin's are the same for all of us
one heartbeat, one fire
callin' us home, see

Born Again Indian

each morning he lights the sacred medicines
in the abalone bowl and walks
every inch of his home with blessings
and prayers for peace and prosperity
health and well-being and with gratitude
for everything that already is

he eases the sacred smoke over everything
the drum, the rattle, the rocks
and everything he's collected
that reminds him of the relationship
he has with Earth — *Aki* in his talk
and thanks her for her blessings

standing at the window that overlooks
the lake nestled in the cut of mountains
he feels the sky holding it all in place
and the land singing in its grasp
so that when he closes his eyes he feels
the notes trill within him

now and then he goes to the sweat lodge
to sing and meditate and pray and maybe
cry for things that continue to hurt
and to feel the waves of that ancient heat
purify, rejuvenate and elevate him
to a state where he can carry on

he doesn't dance, doesn't carry a pipe
or wear his hair in braids or a pony tail
or adorn his truck or hats or home
with displays of eagle feathers, buffalo skulls
or the ceremonial trappings that have come
to mean native pride these days

instead there's prayer ties in the corners of the
four directions of his home and a pair of blankets
elders wrapped his wife and him within one time
when they brought stories back to the people
that visitors wrap about themselves and feel
the sacred nature of that gift

he's got an Indian name and he carries teachings
that elders gifted him with on his travels
and he passes those teachings on in the work he does
because they told him that this is how you honour
the gifts that come to you and make you
bigger inside, stronger somehow and proud

so he goes about the process of being Indian
oblivious to fashion and any need to present
an image of himself with books or art or relics
because he's learned to carry ancient paintings
splashed on the caverns of his being
and be content in the knowledge that they're there

and all of that's funny because in the beginning
when he finally made it home
and surrounded himself with Indian things
and learned to talk his talk and walk
a ceremonial road and dance and sing and pray
his own people laughed and called him a Born Again

those voices hurt and cut him deep with shame
and a sense of guilt that he hadn't learned
anything about himself while he was growing up
even though they knew he'd been swept away
and made to live alone with his skin
in a world that was not his own

so when he made it back against all odds
he wanted this living connection to who he was
so desperately that he celebrated openly
letting the joy he felt flow outward
in the dances, songs and ceremonies and the hair
he grew out and braided to honour all he'd learned

but they laughed and called him Born Again
because he fumbled with the pipe and struggled
to pronounce his name and pray in his Ojibway talk
apple, they said sometimes, with the white inside
and the red skin on the outside tacked on
almost like an afterthought

it took a long, long time to get over that
and it was only the elders that came to guide him
that showed him that what it really meant
to be an Indian these days was to present yourself
openly and earnestly to the spiritual way
and be "borne again" to the heart of it

so he stands content and watches the sun break
over the crest of the mountains across the lake
offers a pinch of tobacco to the spirit of Creation
asaama nee-bah gid-eenah, he says in prayer
I offer tobacco today — then he looks up at his home
and walks inside to find himself again

Geographies

If time and life were to take my eyes I could navigate our
home's geography by feel. Braille it. Read it with the tips
of my fingers and the wide flush pasture of my palms and
never knock a knee or jar a toe against any of the small juts
and peninsulas of our living. Lord knows I've practised it
enough. Moonless nights when sleep laid claim to you
I've crept across the creaking boards to sit at the window
overlooking the mercury platter of the lake as coyotes yip
on the ridge behind us and the sudden streak of an owl
flays back the skin of night above our yard. Or the noise
of something moving beyond the walls has called me from
our bed and I've stalked it window to window, skulking like a
thief and felt this space tattoo itself to my skin. I can walk the
length and breadth of this place in darkness and never feel
the lack of light. Geographies become us when we inhabit
them enough. And so I enter every room skin first, the wash
of the smell of our being here borne on currents of air like
motes of dust, settling everywhere at once, leading me back to
you again with every sure and practised placing of the foot.

Pacific Rim

for Debra on her forty-eighth birthday

indiscernible
this line formed by the great
overturned bowl of the sky
horizon suggested
as the eagle's cry
suggests sound

there's a basso profundo to the crash of surf on rocks
rumbles of strange mariner tales or whale story
carried by current and retold by tide
elegant
passionate as the embrace of starfish to rock
or eerie and enchanted as the anemone's grasp
a siren's call living in gentle, waving cilia
tidal hair
the mermaid's dance in water filled
with singing

there's nothing here to suggest the life
or lives we left behind us
only sound and air and histories spoken
in the sudden spray of heron from a tree
or this rock cupped in your hand

shellfish left behind a symbol for us
not of emptiness or departures or even loss
but of being
it's what we leave behind for those that follow
that counts in the end
that's crustacean wisdom

the mother of pearl shimmer of truth
that lives on our shelves now
alongside the rocks and wood and nets
and floats and curios
adrift to adorn our world

I don't know what it is about this place
that makes such perfect sense
only that geographies sometimes
need our hearts to fill them
as though this delicate joining of spirit to sky
were the underpinning of everything

you fit here

you fill space
as easily as this ragged seam
of coastline fills the eye
rendering distance and forgetting
to timelessness as simple, as pure and perfect
as the line a seagull makes
sailing across the sky

when I think of this continent's edge now
this surrendering to ocean
I will think of myself as coastline
eased, affirmed and recreated
by virtue of you washing over me
the surf of you
filled with stories and bearing news
of other worlds beyond my own
adding to me
this beach of my being
you adorn with treasures

Dreamwoman

For the longest time I believed
that Dreamwoman would be the one
who cared that the starting infield
for the 1965 Boston Red Sox
was Thomas, Mantilla, Petrocelli and Malzone
or that Bob Mosley was
the bass player for Moby Grape
or that the banjo harkened back
to a gourd strung with strings
from Africa's Gambra River
or that the word carousel comes
from the French word *carrousel*
meaning a playful tournament of knights
or that the thirteen central poles
on a tipi each stand for a specific principle
to guide the lives of those who
lived there

I thought Dreamwoman
would care deeply
about all of that
and take it as important
but it turns out instead
that she simply cares
that I do

Elder 2

to the memory of Jack Kakakaway

sometimes he'd just walk away
from the car and head out
across Kananaskis through the trees
and up the slope of a mountain
or along the ragged seam of a creek
where whitefish finned in pools
and the smell of cedar wafted
over everything and I would
follow waiting
for the words to fall

he'd stop now and then
and just look at things
or reach out a hand
to touch moss or stone
and nod and offer up
a half smile or close
his eyes and lift his face
to the frail breeze
and breathe

he put his hand in a bear print once
and knelt there praying
silently
and when he laid tobacco down
beside a mountain spring
I did it too
wordlessly
and he smiled

and I remember how after
one long afternoon of quiet
rambling through the hills
he stood beside the car
and looked back across the land
raised his hands and bowed
his head then looked up
square at me and asked
"did you hear all that?"

and the funny thing is
I did

Grandfather Talking 3 — On Time Passing

Fifty years ago now there wasn't nothing like this nowhere.
Me I'm lying in a bed in a room in a brick building they call a
retirement home but me I never had nothin' to retire from.
The bush an' the river an' the land don't ask the Anishinabeg
to punch no time card and there was never no boss man
there when I done things to put no cash in my hand. So me
I figger retirement means to be put away somewhere like
they put me here on accounta my hands don't work so good
no more with the arthritis and me I know I couldn't walk
the bush now even if I wanted to — and I do, my boy. I do.
But they bring me a beer every now and then I keep under
my mattress so the nurse can't see, drink it long and slow,
hold it in my mouth and taste it good. Ever good them beer
sometimes. Make me remember. Like that time me and old
Stan Jack standin' on the dock at the Gun Lake Lodge watchin'
that sun go down, both of us noddin' and not speakin' on
accounta us we see things like that us Ojibway and there's no
words big enough to say. We drunk beer slow there him and
me. One each. Just happy watchin' the land and feelin' all
easy with each other like you come to when you know a man
long time. Him he's gone now old Stan but us we used to
walk together outta Whitedog into the bush an' out onto the
land to places where they never had no names for them on
accounta us we never needed no names. You hold a place in
your memory for what it gives to you. Call it somethin' you
change it and us we never wanted to change nothing out
there. Us we knew our way around by feel like. Where the
wind comes through a gap, how rapids sound, how the voice
of them is diff'rent comin' from the east than from the west,
the cool you feel on your face steppin' into the shadow a
ridge throws all on you. Yes, that land it's a feeling, my boy.
Or least it was one time. But them they come and put in
roads. Pretty soon there's houses. Big cut lines through the

trees. There's diff'rent kind of memories for the people then. For me too. Gotta remember which road takes you to which lake 'steada followin' the trees. Me I went from that dock in the sunset to the truck the old man got and drivin' to Kenora that one time in '59 and seein' a girl looking for a ride to town an' pullin' over and her climbing up into the cab of that old truck and grinnin' at me with a face like sunshine an' us talkin' like old friends and when we made the curve at Minaki how she touched my leg an' we both smiled, me showin' more gum than Safeway. Stayed in town four days that time. First time I ever forgot the bush me. First time I ever knew I could. Funny huh, how fast something like a truck and a girl an' town can change you? Change everything?

For Generations Lost

Against the sky the trees poke crooked fingers
upwards in praise
and even the rocks lie lodged like hymns
on the breast of Earth
way hi ya hey way hi

I sing for you
even though my language feels foreign on my tongue
and the idea of myself
scraped raw and aching from years of absence
has only now begun to form itself into a shape I recognize

I watch you wander across the skin of this planet
bearing wounds that seep poison into your blood
your faces drawn into masks like the spirit dancers wear
to chase away the night
way hi ya hey way hi

when I returned to you I never thought of this
a people like me who had to fight
to reclaim themselves
but I've come to like this even more
love you for the pain you bear like saints
the history of your displacement
tattooed upon your faces
in lines and wrinkles etched like songs
in a lower register
sung from the gut

and yet you dance
you walk the Red Road of the spirit
and become more of who you were created to be
despite the incursions and the invasions
of your minds and bodies and souls
it's a struggle perhaps
but I've watched you reclaim yourselves
one ravaged piece at a time, mend and succeed
despite all odds to remain warriors
who dance the sun across the sky
and sing the rain down upon the land
way hi ya hey way hi

there is so much strength in you
and I want to tell you that if you break
do it moving forward not away
risk everything
for the real victory is the journey itself
and the only thing we take away or leave behind
is the story of that trek
to be told and retold forever
on the tongues of those we love

you taught me that
in your lodges and your teachings you showed me
that the world remains a wild place
and our only choice is harmony
way hi ya hey way hi

I can't replace the years they took away from you
salve the bruises and the scars they left upon your skin
heal the seeping wounds you carry after all these years
or return the disappeared ones to your arms
I can't erase that past
but I can learn to dance and I can learn to sing
in the language that has always been my own
I can celebrate in the ceremony and the ritual
they could never take away
become in my own way
the expression of you
before the darkness fell
and after the light returned
as it does now
where warriors dance the sun across the sky
and sing the rain down upon the land
way hi ya hey way hi

Ojibway Graveyard

Beyond here is the residential school where
hundreds of our kids were sent sprawling
face first against the hard-packed ground
of a religion and an ethic that said "surrender"
and when they couldn't or wouldn't
they wound up here just beyond the gaze
of the building that condemned them to
this untended stretch of earth

everywhere
the unmarked graves of a people
whose very idea of god sprang from
the ground in which they're laid

there is no fence here no hedgerow
to proclaim this as a sanctuary or even
as a resting place only bitter twirls
of barbed wire canted wildly on posts
rotted and broken and snapped by neglect
unlike the marble and granite headstones
that proclaim the resting places of nuns
and priests devoted to the earthly toil
of saving lost and ravaged souls
for a god and a book that says
to suffer the children to come
unto the light that never really
shone for them
ever

even the wind is lonely here
clouds skim low and the chill
becomes a living thing that invades
the mind and there is nothing
not even prayer in any human tongue
that can lift the pall of dispiritedness
created here for them to sleep in

a brother's grave somewhere in the rough
and tangle of the grasses can't be seen
only felt like a cold spot between the ribs
and a caught breath sharp with tears

bitterness
what they slipped onto the tongues
of generations removed from us
like a wafer
soaked in vinegar

they say we Indians never say goodbye
but I doubt that's true
no people in their right minds or hearts
would cling to these sad effigies
the knowledge that someone once thought
that they were less than human
deserving nothing in the end
but an unmarked plot of earth
beneath a sullen sky the weeds and grasses
stoked by wind to sing their only benediction

we bid goodbye
to nuns and priests
and schools
that only ever taught us pain

keep your blessing for yourselves
in the end you're the ones
who need them

Ojibway Dream

There's nothing like a can of Spam mixed
with eggs, canned potatoes and a mug of
campfire coffee with the grounds still in
cooked over an open flame
and even if there was it wouldn't measure `
up to the crucial test of how it tastes
on bannock made on a stick
that's just the plain truth of things
well, a pickerel packed in clay and tossed
into the fire comes awful close
as long as there's greens and wild mushrooms
tossed over flame and then blueberries
all washed down with Ojibway tea
then a smoke to share
with the Spirits might
just come close
but then again a nice moose rubaboo
properly done with flour, water and maple
syrup with bannock for dipping is hard
to resist at the best of times provided
there's a cob of corn roasted on the fire
with the husk still on and water from
the river cold and rich with the mineral taste
that reminds you of rocks and lakes upstream
and time and the fact that the way
to an Ojibway man's heart
isn't through his stomach
but through his recollections
while seated on a cheap red stool
in a plastic diner looking out
over a freeway choked with cars
and people hungering
for something better tasting
than success

Copper Thunderbird

in memory of Norval Morrisseau

Diogenes you said went walking
with a lamp in the broadest daylight
in a search for one good man
as though that would explain how
they came to find you lurking
in the bushes beyond Hastings & Main drunk
that early summer of '87
raving and talking in ebullient colours
as though the air were a canvas
and legends are born on the dire breath
of rot-gut sherry and the twisting snake
of dreams bred in the bruise of hangover mornings
where Diogenes wakes to crawl
on hands and knees into the light himself

you chuckled then
said they'd never get you
and the truth is they never did

in the belly of legends lives
the truth of us
where shape-shifters walk and flying skeletons
cruise the long nights of our souls
and the tricksters inhabit the dark
where the light of the lamp
you shone there bleeds fantastic colour
into the crevices we've learned
to be afraid to look into for fear
we'd see ourselves peering outward
and know we needed you or your like
to paint us home

you talked to me of birch bark scrolls
and your grandfather's cabin in the trees
where the map of our being laid out in pictographs
was translated in the talk you said
was the original talk of our people
that's rarely spoken anymore
then chuckled again and held me fast
with obsidian eyes that gleamed
with teachings and spoke softly of the stories
that came to fill the canvas of you
resplendent in the harmony and sheen
of colours you said were meant to heal
mystic tones and the hue of shaman songs
the river of black becoming the contrast
that teaches us everything about ourselves
if we're willing to bob in its current

so you set them there in the weft and weave
of canvases despite those Ojibway who claimed
that you gave too much away
even though they could only ever guess
at what you meant to say
because they'd closed their ears and hearts
and minds to stories alive
in the belly of legends

you said to me then
"they'll never get me"
and the truth is they never did

all through that long day ensconced
in the feigned rusticity of the Jasper Lodge
you made me tea and told me
the migration story of my people falling
into the old talk every now and then
but I never minded because it was authentic
and the dip and roll of Ojibway became

another way to enter it together
keep it
close to me like the migis shell
you pressed into my palm

when I made it to the ocean eventually
I left it there
returned it to the place of its beginnings
and watched while the surf rolled it over
and over again until it disappeared
like the brush when it's lifted
at the end of the line

I don't know why it is, Morrisseau
that we come to cling to stories so
only perhaps that something in us understands
that what we get from reality sometimes
is only the veneer, the fixative perhaps
that holds everything in place so the art
can happen underneath it all forever

Copper Thunderbird, you said to me
tell the story for the story's sake
let the line lead them where it will
and don't forget that the best ones come
from everything that's gone before
so never be afraid to splash
enough colour to wake them up to that
and in that way, you said
they'll get you in the end
and the truth is
they sometimes do

In Peigan Country 1993

You drive west out of Calgary
swing left at Bragg Creek to the east and down
through Millarville then due south again
letting the blacktop lead you through Turner Valley
while Van Morrison sings something about
travelling himself and with the windows open
the svelte jump of rhythm and blues
gets punctuated by the sudden cry
of a red-tailed hawk skimming across the highway
and the black comma of a bear
eating berries on a hill

you've come to love this drive
the unnecessary westward loop of it
you take just because it feels so good
to motor through this country
that rollicks with good cowboy humour
and rolls with the solemnity
of a well-told tribal tale
this ancient sea
crumpled up into foothills

at Turner Valley you swing west again
and climb into the arms of the Rockies
and you've switched to Leos Janacek now
letting the romantic swirl of violins
ease you upward so that
rounding a curve you look out across
the great purple stretch of prairie
and the sloping curve of the planet
framed by clouds and the ghostly echo
of the pounding hooves of Peigan ponies
chasing buffalo to the cliff in the gully
where women wait with knives and clubs
and honour songs to take the sacred meat
of their older brother and join it
to their own

the road bends into grizzly country
and there's a long sloping downward curve
between the hump of twin ridges
and where it levels out there's the sudden
smell of medicine sage from a meadow
flat as a table
and you ease the car to the shoulder
clamber out and squint across the wide green
to the resolute grey and weathered face
of the granite cliffs at its southern edge
there's a packet of tobacco in the trunk
and retrieving it you set out across
this perfect meadow while ground squirrels
voice their irritation at your presence
and the smell of sage is so sharp
you can feel it in your lungs

at the far end the ground drops off at your feet
and there's the gorge in a narrow
vertical drop to the river twisting
into rapids and pools far below
and the sage is growing thick as hair
on the sheer slope of it

so you offer tobacco and a prayer
and bend to gather this sacred medicine
and you can hear the river and the wind
and the voices of the squirrels
and the swish of the meadow grasses
like the whisper of fancy-dance shawls
and young girls' feet kicking gracefully
to the beat of a drum
and you lose yourself so completely
in the timeless feel of this act of gathering
that when the wind picks up you smell
the rain and there's a sudden bank of clouds
pushed in low above the cliffs
with the roll of thunder and the smell of lightning
and you stand and just for a second
in the middle of that meadow
you see a circle of tipis
and the people dancing

but there's a flash of lightning
and the vision winks out
and you're stood there
on the precipice
with an armful of sage
feeling honoured
and blessed and a little weak in the knees
but happier than you've ever been

walking back across that meadow
the rain pelts down and you lift your face
so that it can wash you
and reaching the car you tuck the medicine away
and turn to the rain again
and dance shirtless
in that meadow where the people came
in the Long Ago Time to sing and celebrate
this power you feel all around you

and in that rain and in the presence
of the vision you took for real
you came to realize that freedom
is the shrugging off of worldly things
and that in the ceremony of that
lies a common practical magic
that's not so much Indian as it is human
an ordinary thing we lose
when we cease believing in things
like dancing shirtless in the rain
medicine and ceremony and prayer
and the ability of the planet to show us things
she keeps sheltered in her breast

driving home you listened to the music
of the medicine on the seat behind you
the sage, the women's power
grandmother teachings
holding everything together

The Trouble with Indians

The trouble with these Indians he says, is they want everything for nothing. There follows a clamour of grunts and the thump of beer glasses hitting the table and you can tell by the look of him that he's just hitting his stride. The other thing, he says, is that they blame us poor schmucks for what went down in our great-great-grandfather's time, like we gotta shell out now for what happened then. This land claim business and this treaty rights business and the whole reconciliation thing? It's all about money anyhow and me I don't figure there's a way for anybody to buy their way back into the past. But you get those brown fuckers started and all they want to talk about is their grandfather and how if things were now like they were then we'd all be better off. I call BS on that. Before we came they had nothin'. They weren't even using the land they lay claim to now. There's a round of "amen to that," "give 'er straight," and "friggin' A." And someone shouts across the room for another round and the guy settles into his chair and meets everybody's eye before he starts in again. We give 'em guns and money, steel and liquor and an invitation to the future and all they could ante up was a toboggan, snowshoes and an ear or two of corn. We give them religion, education, government, reservations and no frickin' taxes and all they can do is whine about someone stealing their land when they weren't lookin'. They get every friggin' thing for free, free house, free health care, free university, free land, free jobs at the damn band office and still no frickin' taxes and they still whine about what they lost. But they can drink our liquor, screw our women, claim our rightful property, sue our government for cash they don't try to earn in any kind of respectful way and then they go and tell the world how bad they're done by here. He stands up and holds a hand over his heart and belts out a line or two in a big bass voice.
"O Canada," he sings. "Your home's on native land." Everyone

laughs like hell, even the waitress who drops him a free one. When he sits back down there's big, hearty, manly slaps on the back and shoulders and he basks in it, swallows half his beer and grins like a silly kid who farted at the table. You can always tell an Indian, he says, pauses and looks everybody in the eye, holds the moment, savours it, then says, can't tell 'em much . . . and laughter rocks the place again. He flicks his watch up to his face, and drains off his beer and stands to hitch his pants and straighten his suit. "Been fun but I gotta work," he says and turns to leave. "Where you workin' anyway?" someone asks. He turns at the door and levels a grin at everyone. "Indian Affairs," he says and his belly laugh follows him out into the world.

Medicine Wheel

I

When you come to stand upon the land there's a sense in you
that you've seen it all before. Not in any empirical way. Not
in any western sense of recognition but in the way it comes
to feel upon your skin, the way it floods you with recollection.
Standing here beside this tiny creek in the mountains you
suddenly remember how it felt to catch minnows in a jar.
The goggle-eyed sense of wonder at those silvered, wriggling
beams of light darting between stones and the feel of the
water on your arms, cool and slick as the surface of dreams.
You lived your life for the sudden flare of sunlight when
you broke from the bush back then and the land beckoned
through your bedroom window so that sometimes when the
house was dark and quiet you stood there just to hear the call
of it spoken in a language that you didn't know but that filled
you nonetheless with something you've grown to recognize
as hope. So that you came to approach the land like an old
familiar hymn, quietly, respectfully, each step a measure, each
breath a softly exhaled note. That creek ran out of farmland
and wound its way to the reservoir behind an old mill, the
voice of it a chuckle, its edges dappled by the shadows of old
elms and its light like the dancing bluish-green eyes of the
girl on the bus you could never find a way to say a word to. So
you lay across a long flat stone to dip a mason jar elbows deep
and hung there, suspended in your boyhood, while minnows
nibbled at your fingertips and the breeze brought moss and
ferns and rot and scent of cows and flowers to you and you let
that arm dangle until the feeling went away then raised it with
minnows frantic in the sudden absence of their world. Oh,
you couldn't keep them. Couldn't carry them home like a
carnival prize, give them names or place them in a bowl upon
your desk. No, something in you understood even as a boy of

twelve that some things ache to be free and the charm of
them resides in their ability to be that freedom. So you let
them go. Let them swim away. But when you rose you carried
something of that creek, that cold against your arms, the
sun-warmed stone against your belly, the breeze, the light and
the idea of minnows, away with you forever. So that standing
here at fifty-five on the edge of another laughing creek you're
returned to that place, and you're surprised to find it here
like the feeling of opening your eyes after sleep and finding
home all around you once again. It's a journey, this life.
A crossing of creeks on stepping stones where so much comes
to depend on maintaining balance on every careful placing
of the foot.

II

weweni bizindan
omaa ashi awe asemaa
listen careful
put the tobacco here

lay it soft upon the Earth and pray
say great thanks to your Mother
for everything she gives to you
and walk this way
in the path of the sun across the sky
for this is the trek
we all must make
so that we can gather medicine
to make this life a ceremony
anami'aawin — a prayer
to all that is
and everything that will be
upon our journey's end

a great walking
this path whose final gift
is vision

III

them they call it the medicine wheel but us
we never had no need for wheels
so it's always been a sacred circle
then and now for us
see, wheels my boy, had to be invented
and this was always just a gift to people
something that always was
and always gonna be
on accounta Spirit made it

them teachin's never come from us
but we come to own them
when we make the journey

pass 'em on then
make sure to honour
the gift they are that way

that's the medicine way, my boy
gwekwaadziwin — respect
just knowin' that everything and everyone
has their place here
and us sometimes we need to help
each other find our way

if that's a wheel
me I hope it keeps on turnin'

IV

you lie on this slant of hillside
staring up at a sky dimpled
with the light of countless
possible worlds
and it feels like you're impaled
on it somehow
the motion of the planet
the tilt and whirl and spin of it
easing you upwards
back into star dust

Star People came once a long time ago
to sit at the fires of the Anishinabeg
and bring stories and teacher talk
that filled their world with dreams
the Old Ones say they were a gentle sort
and they brought the idea of ceremony
like a great and ancient light

and medicine was born

we all of us are energy they said
we all of us are dream and story
and in the end we return to it
to energy, to spirit, to the great
ongoing tale of our becoming
because there is no end, no finality
only a sacred circle spinning
within us
the spirit place we're meant to travel to
to find the truth of us, the song
we carry forward into dream
sung into story, sung into light
sung into spirit that comes to join
the energy of all things, the completeness
of that sacred circle spinning everywhere at once

all things coming true
together

the circle is wholeness
whose first principle is equality
that creates harmony
that creates the balance
that comes to mean
the humility that transcends all things
that itself evolves into the love
that's born within and reflected out
to keep the circle spinning

they left us then
returning to the place of all beginnings
as the old ones say
and we began the journey to ourselves
the circle of us turning
into years into time into the history
of our time here

the story of us
all we ever have
all we carry with us
and all we leave behind

so you lie on a slant of hillside
against a bowl of stars
the earth pressed against your back
and the feel of that immense fullness
everywhere around you breathing
it into you until you rise finally
to make your way back
to whatever location held you in place
long enough for you to feel
lonely for the sky

V

You come to fifty-five like you came to thirteen. Expectant as a pup at the door waiting for someone to kick it open and send you galumphing out into the world again all legs and lungs and joy. That's the trick of it, really. That's what they mean when people say medicine wheel. Wisdom turning into itself again. The journey we make that brings us back to the only place it can — the place of all beginnings — the innocence we are born in and the great, wide, all-encompassing wisdom of that. You get to be a boy again, charmed by the simple, the ordinary, the commonplace and seeing magic in it. You'd make that journey anytime and the wonder of it lies in bringing others with you, sharing it, offering it to other travellers lost without a light. So you stand looking upward at the sky together then, the awe you feel in bringing energy together, the sacred circle of you, joined by an everyday glory you only need to breathe to recognize, to haul into you to join, to hold in your chest like a wish that frees you. Great wheel, spin, spin.

Nets

you stand on the shore
of the Winnipeg River
and watch the old men smoking
laughing and mending nets
their hands moving
almost by themselves
and when they look up
and see you there
they smile
their hands continuing
the dance they've learned
by touch

this is what it means
to be Indian, you say, Ojibway
the effortless, almost mindless
mending of the nets
we cast across
the currents of time

Powwow

See them dance
against the slow
and even movement of the sky
so that to the eye
colours shift against
the grass and the drum
and the rattle of elk teeth
the swish of shawl, and the clatter
of bells on leggings becoming
the smile on young kids' faces
and the wistful grins of the old ones
sitting back in wheelchairs now
wishing they might dance again
to join the whirling, swirling, stomping, glee
of this great wheel of regalia danced
so that energies might become a blessing
and a prayer bestowed upon this sacred earth
where a simple song sung with drums
sends waves of light across
the universe to that spiritual place
where we all began our journeys
toward this place
where it all comes together
like a vision that travels in
a circle of prayer
to encircle all who
come
     here
       now

Trickster Dream

Crow came to my room last night
dressed in a checkered western shirt
and boots and jeans too tight in the rump
so that he squawked soprano
and groused vociferously
about the lack of a proper avian line

he's hip to things like that
Crow gets around, you know
him and Coyote, well
they've been known to carouse
something awful in the streets of Milan
and even though no one likes
a knock-down loaded Trickster much
they've got a fashion sense to die for
all that fur and feather accessorizing
to go with the Pucci (Coyote's call) scarves
and the Salvatore Ferragamo calf-skin
bag that Crow adores because he
can't hack the shoes
(they don't call them crow's feet for nothing
is how he says it)

anyhow, Crow was on the lookout for Raven
whom he'd heard had been seen
in the vicinity and needed
some advice on metaphor or allegory
aphorism or some such Trickster trick
because he had a gig in Kasabonika Lake
and them Oji-Crees up there
had heard all his schtick before
and the kids were even using
his best lines in the schoolyard now

Crow was after belly laughs
and Coyote couldn't help much with that
on account of he always wanted
to make them howl
although he did have some of the
snappiest zingers in the Trickster biz
and Crow himself had busted a gut
every now and then when Coyote
let loose with those moonlight
prowl stories of his
Raven knew the ins and outs of Trickster-ism
he'd even hung with the big guys
Nanabush and Wesakechak
creating mayhem in a tamarack bog
and driving the local Cree kids wacko
just before they drove south in
a battered '57 Chevy
to dig the crazy Cajun food
in N'aw Lins before Katrina

so he knew a thing or two

Crow hopped from the dresser
to the window ledge and fluffed
his inky feathers in the moonlight
and laid the full force of his
beady obsidian eyes on me
and cackled and croaked
and wondered if we had
any jalapeno-stuffed olives in the house
or the new Black Crowes CD
because Tricksters gotta stay hip
you know
it's where the best bits come from

so I told him that this wasn't
really Raven country but that
there were a lot of crows around
if he wanted to ask

"any nesting in the sunshine?" he asked
I asked him why and he wriggled his shoulders
in the red-checkered shirt
and hiked the jeans up some
"always on the lookout for a hot black chick,"
he said and mimicked a rim shot
and a cymbal crash

he was right
he was in desperate need of schtick

Mountain Morning

it's so still you can feel
the boundaries of things shimmer
with the effort it takes
to hold themselves in

even the birds are hushed
and in this perfect silence
where not even a faint breeze strays
the idea of manitous
hovered over everything
becomes the first wavered light
of the sun through the clouds
and the storm that gathers to the west
announces itself
in a fanfare of silence

small wonder, you say
that there's no word
for "power" in your language
only *spirit*
only *medicine*

but then
there's no word for "obvious"
either

On Battle Bluffs

for Jennifer and Ron Ste. Marie

they say that in the old days
the scouts would come to sit and watch
for any sign of enemies coming
out of the purple mountains
or across the hard iridescent platter
of the lake

from this height the land
stretches out across the territory
of the Secwepemc, the Shuswap
as it's said in the settler talk
and there's history in the sudden flare
of space, the country below us reduced
to angle and a narrowing where the lake
pulls our focus forward into the hard vee
of its disappearing
so that it becomes like time, really
wending, winding, curving in upon itself
turning into something else completely
while we breathe the exhalations
of the breath of those who came
and went before

wind on stone
the clock of us ticking
relentlessly

I can hear the cries of battle rising
upward on drafts of air
just as I feel the solemn peace
that fell over young men who sat for days here
praying, fasting, seeking the vision
that would lead them into manhood
perhaps becoming one of those who fell
beneath the hammered blows of conflict
amidst the clumps of medicine sage
on the sere grasslands below
it's a sacred place because of that
this place of becoming and leaving
this warrior place where the spirit of a people
resides in wafts of air
risen from their territory to climb beyond
here to the place of old voices
whose home is the wind

eagle wings skimming
silently across
this hallowed blue

lying against the ancient rock
feeling the push of it on my back
the sun bakes everything in radiant waves
that shimmer and dance
so that looking out across the battlefields below
the land itself weaves into motion
the sun dance maybe
or another act of being

I don't know why places like this
affect me so
only that the search for a sense
of my own history involves many histories
the sum of us lodged within these sheer bluffs
so that coming here becomes a pilgrimage of sorts
a deliberate marching, plodding, shuffling forward
and backwards at the same time
to reclaim a piece of me
I didn't know existed
this rock a vertebrae
in the great spine of story
of our time here
together

songs rise higher
borne on air
returning

Papers

for Debra

I walk by with another armload and watch you scanning
papers for signs of life. This life that passed. It's funny how
something like a postcard scribbled against the gunwales of
a sloop off Wanganui can come to mean so much. Vague
hieroglyphics cast from the hands of an unknown people,
place and time and distance referenced by what's implied and
not by what you know, a connection you feel as paper in the
hands. Still, you plumb each line and image like a sounder
reading the depth of unknown waters, breathless for the tale
born by echo. There's a lifetime in these boxes, and in their
faded inks and snapshots running to opaque your father's
world fills itself in hint by hint, line by line, detail by detail,
until finally, as the boxes disappear you assemble a keepsake,
a shrine they so inelegantly call a "scrap" book — the only
treasure you can take away. They are the sum of us the things
we keep and in the hands of loved ones once we're gone,
those paper trails of living retain their sense of self, sit there
squarely in the palm, crooning old jazz ballads, moaning a
particular blues, singing their histories.

Getting Supper

there's nothing too traditional
about a tuna steak fashioned
into burgers to someone
with sturgeon as a totem
but you could make the case
that *wasabi* is an Ojibway word
if you said it slow enough

still I've learned to brandish a knife
and I can mince without too much
damage to my manliness
and now that I know there's things to skin
I can retain a savage decorum
even if it's just an onion
and I face the whole
slice and dice thing
like a cavalry charge
over a battlefield of lettuce

but there's something elemental in
the hunkering over a stove or a grill
that hearkens back to fires
glowing orange in the night
and the smell of meat roasting on a stick
so that this whole getting supper thing
has its merits in a purely
cross-cultural way
even if I flunk the miso tuna burger test

the hunter prowls Safeway aisles now
the gatherer chases bargains
in the produce section and hey
shiitake is a ceremonial word you know

honest

Monk at Midnight

They say he learned to play by ear and that by the time he
made it to Minton's he was shellacking the keys with his whole
body as though the fingers splayed in gigantic stretches were
extensions of the spirit he pushed across the room, over the
tables, up to the rafters and down again to explode in the
souls of the ones lucky enough to hear him then. He was a
bear of a man, a grizzled veteran of the road, so that when he
laid down a note it meant more than the timbre of it against
the night, the room, the crowd, it meant a thousand nights
walking alone through darkened streets with shards of sound
borne down from streetlamps, up from the desolate alleys and
sluiced down the gutters and out to the black current of the
river to the sea where jazz is born in the tempest of things
and the toss and tide of fate made manifest in cigar smoke
and whiskey and seven octaves alive in the hands of a genius
who brooked no falsehood in notes or life. Monk played with
his whole body. You could hear that. He played every note in
sheer amazement of the one he'd played before. So that the
cascade of runs made that keyboard sound eighteen feet long
and standing looking out from the window at the shadow of
the mountains in the darkness, Monk, dead as hell for almost
thirty years, reaches out behind you and fills the corners of
the room with sound. Awesome, you think to be touched this
way and jazz becomes an Ojibway thing by virtue of the blues
built into it and the feeling of the moan of a song caught in
the throat and begging release to the land where all things
are born and all things return in the end and the belief we
hold that it can save us, the song spilled out upon the land.
Jazz and soul and hope and harmony and all things Ojibway
becoming one at once, everything alternating a semitone
apart, until the last note fades and you stand there in your
lack, waiting . . .

Paul Lake Fog

Great beards of air
moving slow
stretching as if tugged
by a child's hands
introducing trees
limb by limb
and crows placed
neatly along the power line
like a string of beads
hung around the neck
of the mountain

nothing but the air moves
until the sun intrudes
from the east
to show the deer
watching you from the trees
at the end of the driveway
the smoke of her breath
joined to the fog
leaving

no one ever pulled up
to heaven with a U-Haul
someone told you that once
and if you laughed about it then
here you come to understand
the utter sense of it
that this mosaic of things
the bits and pieces
of this life that move
you so
are what you carry with you
when you go

spirit lives in everything
there are no departures
only another joining

West Arm Kootenay Lake

There's a wind from the southeast pushing
waves up to the edge of the beach
where you can see the full moon hanging
behind a bank of clouds set between
the humped shoulders of mountains
everything is indigo now
even the shadows have retreated to purple
as the silvered mercury of the moon
puts a sheen on the body of the lake

if you look long enough the motion
of the water makes it look as though
the moon were moving, drifting further
away across the depths of space
with the planet giving chase until
you come to feel yourself move
so you spread your arms and close
your eyes to feel the tractive tug of it
calling you forward outward beyond
all sense of where you are until
a part of you becomes moonbeam, star
dust, nebula and the tail of a comet maybe
and you laugh to feel that

it's not very Indian you say
to let yourself escape like this
to wander out across the universe
when all your issues are here on the planet
land claims, treaty rights, the clamour for a
place at the negotiating table on things
that affect us and dammit all Wagamese
there's people starving in Pikangikum
and eighteen people share a two-room house
without a proper toilet in Atawapiskat
and there's kids surrendering to gang life
glue and solvents and their parents
are drunk and can't give a damn
because the chief ran off with a few
hundred grand of the fiscal funding
in the new pickup truck he bought
his nephew's vote with who won't need
it until he gets out of jail anyway
and there's no one watching out
for shit like that even though it happens
everywhere and the people pay the price
as in the suicide rate that still hangs high
above the national average
(though why they even have a stat for that
boggles you at the best of times)

when you open your eyes there's
nothing before you but the land
and in its absolute stillness
there's the sound of wind on water
and as you push to hear it you discover
that you have to really want to
it doesn't just come to you
you have to crave it, yearn for it
ache for the luxuriant whisper that says
harmony happens on its own here

when you come to believe that it fills you
and you become beach and wave and lake
and mountains humped against the semi-dark
and a moon that sails across the sky like hope
another thing you have to really want
in order for it to happen

in the end it's as Indian as it gets
this reaching out to feel connected to imagine
becoming a part of things displaced
from you by issues and bothers and hurt
the Old Ones say that harmony and separation
cannot occur in the same time and place
and maybe that's it
this whole native issues thing
that you ultimately become
what you believe in most
even a planet chasing a moon
across time and space

September Breaks — Paul Lake

The lake exhales a jubilant mist that carries
within it the desperate calls of loons
making preparations to wing south
and there's a bear ambled down
to drink and eye the yards hewn
from mountainside lush with blackberry
late season saskatoons and the trashcan
someone left the lid ajar upon
as an eagle cuts a slice out of the sky
then gives way to the osprey clan
hungry for trout and the muskrat who
claimed a home beneath your friend's dock
noses an expanding vee into the water
placid with chill and the feel of the
mist rising slowly above it all
like silent applause and the eagle
flies into the sun rising in a blunt
cleft between the ribs of
mountains

for the longest time I didn't know
that such a place existed
couldn't believe really
that it could even be imagined
let alone allow me to stand here
at this window with a mug looking
over it all stunned into believing
suddenly that beauty exists somewhere
beyond the vague hope you carry
that you can change the world
with words

you can't really
in the end it's just you
that you adjust to fit the situation
and mornings like this remind you
that ugliness has a reservation
to sit all churlish and smug
waiting for you to disbelieve

but you can't, not now
not after finding the way
this all sits between your ribs beating
like a second heart
calling you from the window
to the desk where you'll sit
and peck away like a frantic rooster
for the words to lift the sun
back into the sky and call September forward
because it's not really fall
when it elevates you so

White Shit

Seventeen without a clue. Wandering like a tourist in my own life, picking up whatever I thought might fit, might flesh me out, give me meaning, when the old Indian across the table at the Mission asked through a mouthful of thin stew and bread, "What's with all the white shit?" Then in stir, six months for stupidity, the native guy with braids and a "*today is a good day to die*" tattoo above his heart leans on the bars of my cage, studies my row of books and asks, "What's with all the white shit?" Then, the girl I wanted so much to love, long flowing black hair, angular face, obsidian eyes and a name like Rain Cloud Woman in her Cree talk, wanders about my room picking up the trinkets and the stuff, eyeing it like relics, squints at the Beethoven records and the Judy Chicago print on the wall, looks at me and laughs and asks, "What's with all the white shit?" They cut me, those words. Sliced clean to the bone, through the fat and gristle of the world to lay open the glistening bone of fact and I studied my brown face in the mirror in the hard yellow slant of the morning sun. "What *is* with all this white shit?" I asked myself. And that's when I turned Indian. That's when I became a born-again pagan/heathen/savage, dancing, singing, turquoise- and buckskin-wearing, chanting, drumming, guttural, stoic, hand-sign talking, long haired, feather wearing, walking-talking iconographic representation of the people, man. There was no room in that for any white shit. But I was young then and hadn't heard the voices and the teachings of my people and hadn't turned my heart to truth. It would take some doing. It would take some isolation and the loneliness that false pride instills and it would take a desperate reaching out to belong somewhere, anywhere, with anyone. Three decades later I have seen some serious shit, man, and life is all about the truth of things. So I sit drinking coffee on a deck overlooking a mountain lake in a community of white folk,

surrounded by computers, a TV, music, books, a pickup
truck, a car, guitar, piano, appliances, conveniences and
responsibilities. But there's an Indian at the heart of me.
I feel him here where the crows speak Ojibway, where the
breeze carries hints of old songs sung around a fire in the
night, where a hint of sage in the air shows me the line where
ancient and contemporary meet, telling me that traditional
and cultural, in the end, becomes where you live, where you
set your soul to rest and I look around at fifty-five and see that
where I am is always where I wanted to be. Life has become
a ceremony and The Indian sans beads, sans feathers, sans
get-ups and trickery surrounded by white shit and glad of it.

Mother's Day

You take me somewhere I have never been before and the immensity of the landscape fills me with wonder. It took me a long time to become the kind of man for whom wonder was a property of being. But you took me there easily like shadows breaking in sunlight. I know you wonder sometimes about your measure, how the world sees you and it's funny because it's you that gives measure to me, and that, I suppose, in the final analysis is what motherhood is all about: the transfer of magic conducted gently like a hand upon the brow. It lives in the eyes of your children when they look at you. Those times when you're not looking, busy with the pots or arranging things, your head bent in concentration, working at getting it right for them. They look at you with eyes filled with wonder. At this woman who bears their chin, their nose, their eyes, their look of solemn thoughtfulness and I see them inhabit the same landscape as I do. All of us transported and transformed by virtue of allowing you to touch us. I love you for that. For the anonymity of motherhood you travel in, oblivious most times to the practical effect of magic you carry in your hands.

To Displaced Sons

In your hands I lay the articles of faith
the elements of this teaching way
that has brought me so far out
of darkness and into the light
of understanding who I am and how
I got to be here as a human being
a man and an Ojibway

that's the thing of it you know
this act of discovery
goes on forever whether
you want to believe that or not
because we're created to be those three things
three truths of us that never change
for the length of time we're here
and our work is the search
for the meaning of those things
so we can carry the teachings on
to where our spirit travels next
on its eternal search
for its highest expression
of itself

this is what our elders say

so that you can never be less
than what you were created to be
you can only become more
and the heart of that teaching means
you never have to qualify for anything
you never have to prove yourself worthy
because you always were
the three truths of you
man, Ojibway, human being
inarguable, inextinguishable, alterable only
by Creator's hand

and she's not likely to

along this path there are many
examples of what it means
to be a good human being
watch for them
and follow their lead
because there are teachers everywhere
even in the most unexpected places
where you wouldn't think to look
they stand there holding mirrors
so that we can see ourselves
and become more

I have found saints in prison cells
and holy women under lamp lights
and great philosophers eating
the humblest fare behind dumpsters
and visionaries in one-room shacks
at the end of gravel roads
burning twigs for warmth
in the very least of these
was always something to carry with me
on the journey to myself

I just had to want to find it

when people learn to live with little
they open themselves up to more
not of worldly things or grandeur
but of spirit
so when the settlers came and saw our people
living simple lives upon the land
they thought us poor and backward
and when we opened our hands
to share the plenty we knew existed
they thought us savage and ill prepared
for a world that demanded fortune
but they were blind to where our ceremonies
directed us
not to a salvation promised on some other plane
but right here on this ground
where we learn to live and become
the people we were created to be

Creator is everywhere around us
we are joined from the moment we arrive
and we sprang from this Earth
so that we can never be lost
we are always home

this is what it means to be
a human being
in the Indian way

it means the world is our teacher
its rhythms and its motions are our university
in the ones who fly
the ones who crawl and swim and walk
four-legged are spirit teachers meant to guide us
and they hold within them
great examples of fortitude, steadfastness
harmony, balance, sharing, loyalty, fidelity
compassion, love, truth, wisdom
and sacrifice
that we need to learn if we are
to learn to live well and long
and take the skin of this planet
as our own

watch them these spirit teachers
they live honestly
for they were born knowing
exactly who and what they are
and have no need of the agony
of the search
they are our protectors
and we honour them by following their natures
seeking to reflect their spirit
in our own
and this is why we call them *dodem*
or totem as the settlers learned to say

in the plants and grasses and even
the rocks are things meant
to inform the way we travel
they teach us of community really
like when the sapling reaches for the sky
from the ribs of the Grandmother tree
when she lies down in the forest
or the stones offering their faces
to the rain so the moss can breathe

in these things are elemental teachings
that bring us to ourselves
that teach us to be human animals
neither less nor more than any other being

this is what the elders say

what we learn is that life is a circle
and the moment that we enter it
the first principle that comes into practice
is equality
for we are energy and we are spirit
and there is no hierarchy there
nor does there need to be
this is why our ceremonies and our rituals
are built on circles
because we are all teachers
because we are all mirrors
because we need each other
to find the truest possible expression
of ourselves

we come out into this reality in humility
naked and crying in the innocence
that allows us to be carried forward into trust
which in turn grows into the strength
that allows us to look within ourselves
for the truth that is our own
and in this way we attain a degree
of the wisdom that allows us to return
to the innocence that bears us
forward into the sacred circle of learning
again for that is what life is
always was
and always will be

there is no end to circles
only continuance
and learning never stops if we allow it

so when we arrive at that point in time
when our joints are old and tired
and we find ourselves aged and bearing
the white in our hair
that is the colour of knowing
we are blessed to find
the greatest teaching waiting for us there
that this journey toward becoming
a good human being, this struggle
results always in our becoming
good men and women
and ultimately good Ojibway
or whoever we were created to be
because we learned the greatest lessons first
when we learned to be good people

I became a good Indian after
I became a good man who learned
to be a good human being
that's the natural way of things
and it can't occur in any other order

so my wish for you is that you learn
to see the world as altar
where everything you need to pray
and sing and hope and dream
and become
is laid out there for your use
when you choose to pick it up
because the truth is, my sons
that's where the power lives
within the choice that we are born with

choose to allow
choose to discover
choose to become more
and in this way you become
a creator
aligned with the spirit of creation
and filled with the immense power
of possibility
the magic that is itself a circle
containing everything

I have learned in my time here
that we are born covered in things
like love and trust and loyalty
humility and hope and kindness
and that sometimes the world
has a way of rinsing those things off us
so we stand naked and crying again
but at that very moment
when we want it the most
Creator allows us to find a way
to re-cover ourselves
in those spiritual qualities

so don't be afraid to fall
it's how we learned to walk
in the first place

instead, go forward in all things
and take the teachings with you
so that in quiet times in quiet rooms
or somewhere out upon the land
you can lay them on the altar again
and choose to pick them up
and carry on

I'll be with you
standing at the edge of a forest somewhere
or on a rock overlooking a stretch of water
breathing and laying tobacco down
in gratitude and mumbling quiet prayers
for the joy of your becoming